For Margaux Cuff-Burnett. – David Long

To my sisters, chị Minh & chị Phương. Thank you for being by my side through the entire "history" of my life, from the very first steps to the most defining moments. – Vinh Nguyễn

To my two furry companions, Mơ & Dưa Lưới. Thank you for being the quiet observers of my life's story. Your presence, your purrs, and even your mischievous antics have made the journey so much more joyful. – Rồng Phạm

HODDER CHILDREN'S BOOKS
First published in Great Britain in 2025 by
Hodder and Stoughton Ltd

Text copyright © David Long 2025
Illustrations copyright © Rồng Phạm & Vinh Nguyễn 2025

David Long and Rồng Phạm & Vinh Nguyễn have asserted their right under the Copyright, Designs and Patents Act 1988, to be identified as the author and illustrators of this work.

All rights reserved. A CIP catalogue record for this book is available from the British Library.

HB ISBN: 978-1-526-36449-4
E-book ISBN: 978-1-526-36450-0

1 3 5 7 9 10 8 6 4 2

Printed in China

Hodder Children's Books
An imprint of Hachette Children's Group
Part of Hodder and Stoughton Limited
Carmelite House, 50 Victoria Embankment London EC4Y 0DZ

An Hachette UK Company
www.hachette.co.uk
www.hachettechildrens.co.uk

The authorised representative in the EEA is Hachette Ireland,
8 Castlecourt Centre, Dublin 15, D15 XTP3, Ireland (email: info@hbgi.ie)

DAVID LONG
RỒNG PHẠM & VINH NGUYỄN

TRACKS THROUGH TIME

The history of the world told through animal adventures

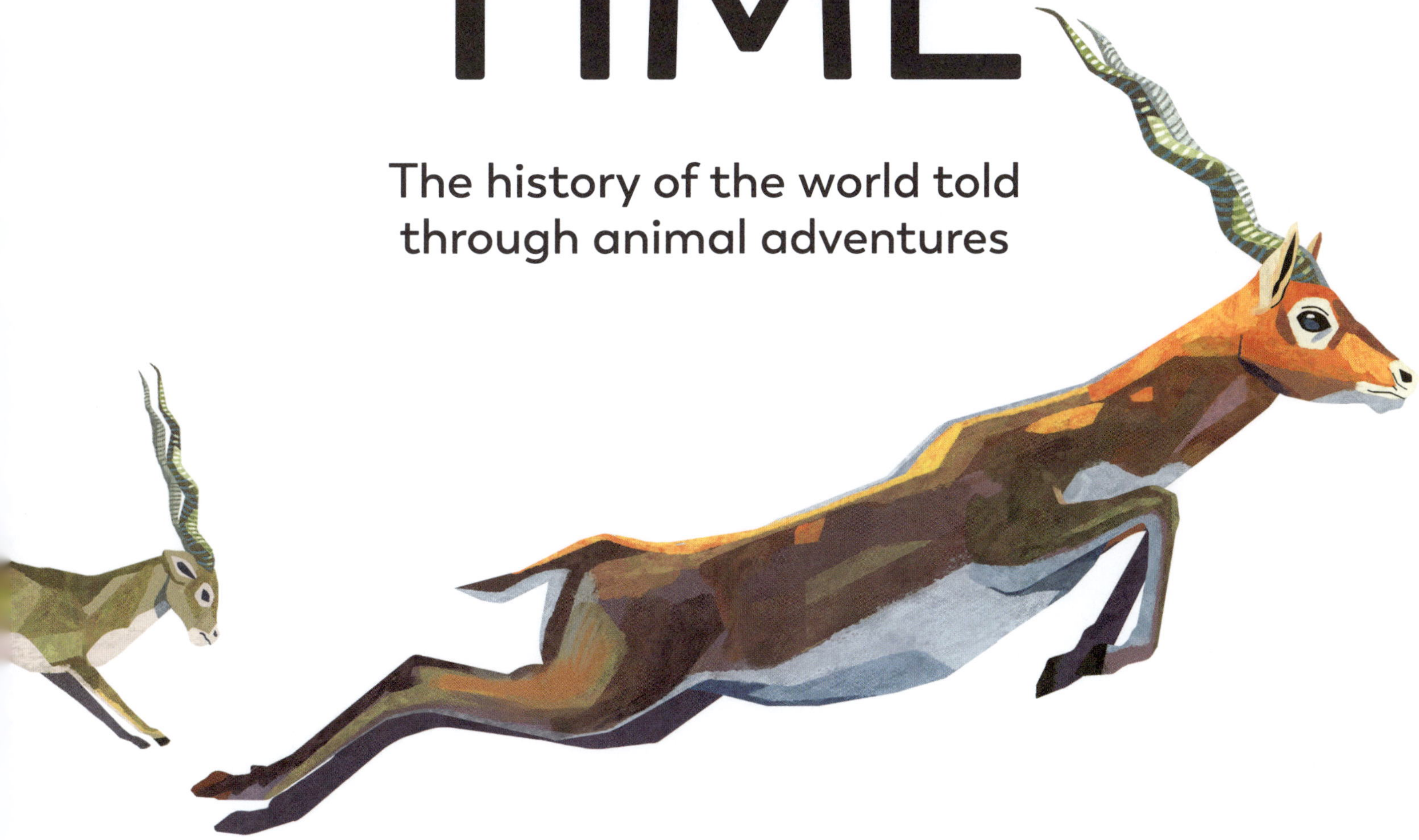

HODDER

Contents

5	Introduction	26	The Fight For Freedom
6	The Human Story Starts Here	28	The Theory of Evolution
8	The Noblest Steed	30	Patriotic Parrot
10	The Rest was Hissstory	32	The World's Worst Dog Walk
12	An Emperor Can't Change His Stripes	34	Survivor Pup
14	Worth His Weight in Gold	36	Deeds Not Words
16	Flea-se Go Away	38	Naval May-ham
18	A Tall Tale	40	A Hero's Flight
20	The Dog who Started a Whole New Church	42	Feline Friend
22	The President's Royal Gift	44	Space Dogs
24	The Pampered Pooch	46	A True Best Friend
		48	Conclusion

Introduction

If animals could talk, the ones in this book would be able to tell you how they met some of the most famous people on the planet and witnessed moments in history that changed the world forever.

These animals were companions and beloved pets, working animals and exotic curiosities. They shared their lives with people from the past: heroes and villains, the rich and powerful, as well as the very poor. The following pages are a chance to see and hear about their extraordinary, exciting real-life adventures and to visit everywhere from ancient Egypt to outer space.

The Human Story Starts Here

TANZANIA · 200,000 BCE

Our greatest enemies used to be lions and leopards. They're quick and they attack without warning. But now . . . now there are much more dangerous creatures roaming these plains: humans. We animals are fast, but humans are so cunning. So dangerous. They hunt as a team. Climbing the trees and hiding in the branches. They attack us as we pass beneath in search of food and water. They're our biggest threat. So shhhhh . . .

Reliable evidence shows that the first humans, our ancestors, lived in Africa. They weren't farmers, so they didn't keep animals or grow crops. Instead, they foraged in groups, looking for edible plants and eating meat from dead animals. They learned how to hunt together and use spears for catching fish and killing larger animals, such as antelope.

Early humans were nomads, which means they moved around to find the food they needed to survive, making camps or finding shelter as they went. They slowly wandered through North Africa and into Asia and Europe. This gradual migration happened over many thousands of years.

Around 11,000 years ago, in a part of the Middle East called Mesopotamia, people first began to settle in villages and towns. The soil was rich and fertile, good for growing crops, so the nomads became farmers. Animals such as antelope were seen as prey, but the farmers began taming animals that could be useful. Over the next few thousand years they learned to keep goats, sheep, cattle, pigs and geese. These animals provided milk, meat and eggs, as well as skins and wool for clothing. In other parts of the world, horses became an important means of transport, and cattle were used to pull ploughs that helped the farmers grow the food.

The Noblest Steed

EUROPE, ASIA, AFRICA · 326 BCE

Bucephalus

Thousands of Indian soldiers stand facing us across the Jhelum River. They look well trained and are heavily armed with spears and arrows, but so are we and we are ready to fight. My master has not lost a battle in more than 10 years and I am certain he will win here too. He has marched us thousands of miles to reach this place, and we have already conquered more land than any army before us. This is why people call him Alexander the Great.

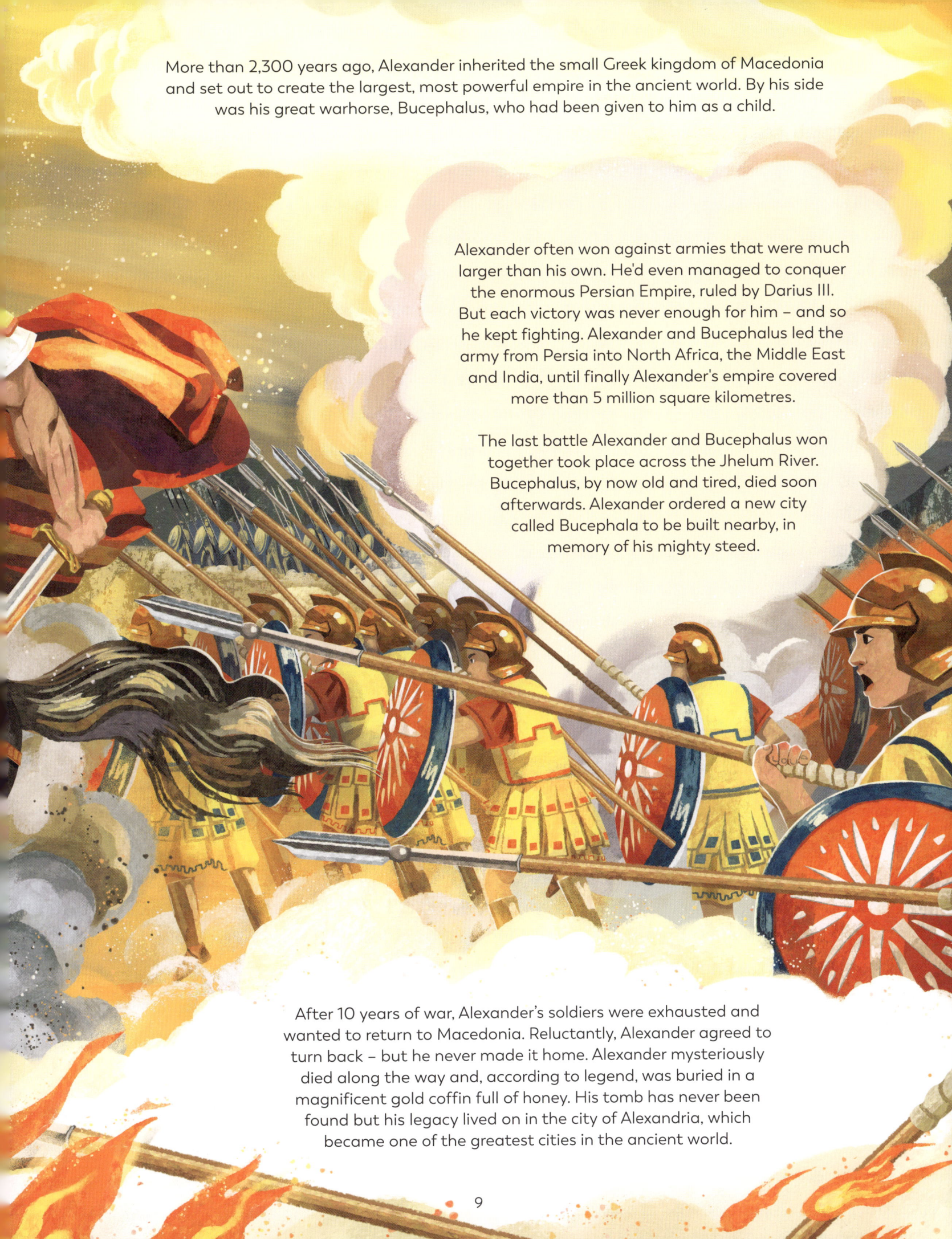

More than 2,300 years ago, Alexander inherited the small Greek kingdom of Macedonia and set out to create the largest, most powerful empire in the ancient world. By his side was his great warhorse, Bucephalus, who had been given to him as a child.

Alexander often won against armies that were much larger than his own. He'd even managed to conquer the enormous Persian Empire, ruled by Darius III. But each victory was never enough for him – and so he kept fighting. Alexander and Bucephalus led the army from Persia into North Africa, the Middle East and India, until finally Alexander's empire covered more than 5 million square kilometres.

The last battle Alexander and Bucephalus won together took place across the Jhelum River. Bucephalus, by now old and tired, died soon afterwards. Alexander ordered a new city called Bucephala to be built nearby, in memory of his mighty steed.

After 10 years of war, Alexander's soldiers were exhausted and wanted to return to Macedonia. Reluctantly, Alexander agreed to turn back – but he never made it home. Alexander mysteriously died along the way and, according to legend, was buried in a magnificent gold coffin full of honey. His tomb has never been found but his legacy lived on in the city of Alexandria, which became one of the greatest cities in the ancient world.

The Rest was Hissstory

EGYPT · 30 BCE

A sssingle bite from me is nearly always fatal. My fangsss are sharp like needles, my poissson killsss my victimsss quickly and quietly. Sssome think thisss is a good way to die. Fassster and lesss painful than a cut from a dagger or a sssword. Sssome people even believe that the great Egyptian queen Cleopatra brought me to her palace ssso that she could kill herssself. No one knows for sure if I really bit her, but the legend made me famousss . . .

Cleopatra was the last great ruler of ancient Egypt, a large and powerful empire that lasted for more than 3,000 years. As a young woman, she had joined with the Roman leader Julius Caesar to defeat her own brother, Ptolemy, and become queen. Her palace was in the great Egyptian city of Alexandria.

Unfortunately, Cleopatra had enemies as well as friends in Rome. A few years later, Caesar was brutally murdered. Cleopatra joined forces and fell in love with another important Roman politician and military leader called Mark Antony. He soon fell out of favour with Rome's new leaders, and Rome declared war on them both. The Romans wanted to add Egypt and its riches to their own growing empire.

Cleopatra and Antony fought the Romans on heavily armed warships just off the coast of Greece. Antony and Cleopatra's navy had thousands of soldiers and at least 200 vessels, but their enemy had hundreds more and an army of skilled archers. The archers fired sharp metal-tipped arrows at the Egyptian soldiers, and within hours nearly all the Egyptian warships had been captured or sunk.

Antony and Cleopatra fled to Egypt, but before long the Roman army invaded. Determined not to be captured by the Romans, Antony stabbed himself.

Shortly afterwards, Cleopatra was found dead in her palace. The story goes that she arranged for a venomous snake to be smuggled into her room in a basket of figs, knowing its deadly bite would kill her.

An Emperor Can't Change His Stripes

ITALY · 65 CE

Phoebe

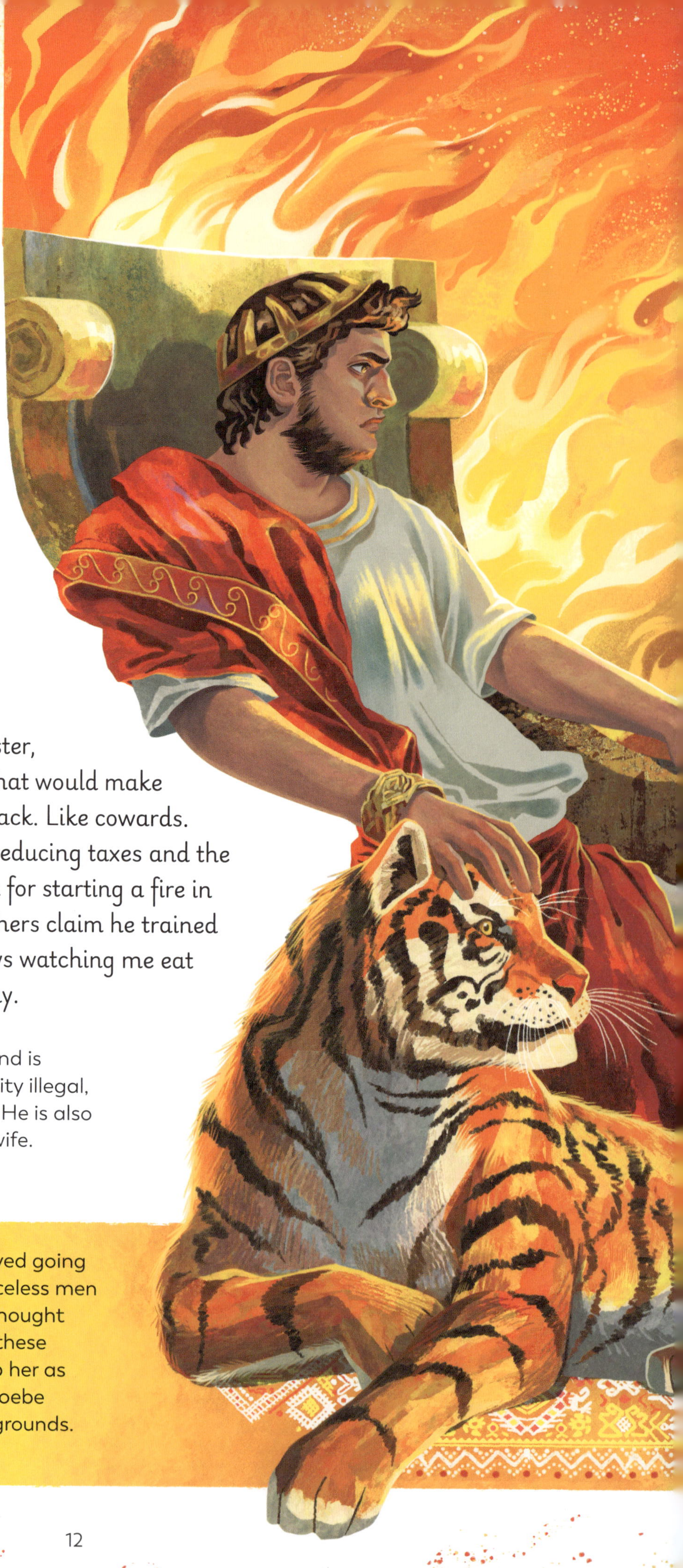

People say terrible things about my dear master, Emperor Nero. Never to his face – because that would make him angry and dangerous – but behind his back. Like cowards. People forget about how much good he did, reducing taxes and the price of food. People would rather blame him for starting a fire in Rome that destroyed hundreds of homes. Others claim he trained me to kill his enemies, and that he even enjoys watching me eat them alive . . . is it true? I couldn't possibly say.

Nero ruled the Roman Empire from 54 to 68 CE and is remembered as a brutal ruler. He made Christianity illegal, and had many Christians tortured and executed. He is also rumoured to have killed his own mother and his wife.

These were very brutal times. Most Romans enjoyed going to gruesome shows in public arenas where defenceless men and women were attacked by wild animals. It is thought that, after seeing a tiger called Phoebe in one of these shows, Nero was so impressed he decided to keep her as a pet. He had a golden cage made for her but Phoebe was often allowed to wander around the palace grounds.

Nero is also known for doing nothing to save Rome when a fire destroyed more than half the city in 64 CE. Hundreds died in the blaze and thousands were made homeless. In those days, fires spread rapidly and were almost impossible to put out because buildings were made mostly from wood.

Nero wasn't even in Rome when the tragedy broke out. But, when he built a huge new palace for himself and Phoebe on top of the wreckage, he was blamed for the fire. Although he had many other public buildings rebuilt, his enemies claimed Nero had started the blaze just to make room for his new palace. This made him more and more unpopular. Eventually, perhaps knowing he was likely to be replaced as emperor, he killed himself.

Worth His Weight in Gold

MALI (WEST AFRICA) · 1324

Thousands of slaves and soldiers are trekking with us towards the holy city of Mecca. The journey is long and tiring. Especially when you're carrying the weight of pure gold on your back. Our master insists we carry the gold so it can be used to build new mosques in the towns and villages that we pass through. He says it is the duty of all Muslims to make the pilgrimage at least once in their lives if they can. Apparently, millions make the journey every year . . . but I don't think everyone does it with as much splendour (or luggage) as Mansa Musa.

Before Mansa Musa's 6,000-kilometre (km) march from Mali to Mecca, in what is now Saudi Arabia, few people outside Africa had even heard of the Mali Empire. It was the largest empire in the world when Musa ruled, and he was probably the richest man who ever lived. He always dressed in expensive coloured silks decorated with gold thread, and even the people he enslaved wore fine uniforms.

Musa's incredible wealth came from mining Mali's rich natural resources that included gold and also salt, which was very precious at this time. People used salt to flavour food and to stop it going off, and Mali had so much of it that in some towns they even used it to make bricks for building their houses.

The Mali Empire grew larger and eventually it covered all or parts of several modern countries: Mali, Mauritania, Niger, Senegal, Côte d'Ivoire, Burkina Faso, Ghana, Guinea, Guinea-Bissau and The Gambia. Mansa Musa owned all of it. His capital city, Timbuktu, became known far and wide as a centre of wealth and learning, because of its mosques, schools, libraries and universities. Today, Mali is one of the poorest countries in the world, but its ancient buildings are reminders of its rich heritage.

Flea-se Go Away

KYRGYZSTAN · 1346

We fleas always seem to get the blame. I promise we never mean to cause any trouble. I've never stung anyone in my life, and I don't have poisonous fangs or huge claws. Plus, I'm tiny. Yet, people say that we've destroyed communities and even brought down entire civilisations. I've heard people say that we're the most dangerous creatures that have ever lived. We are sorry. We never intended to cause harm. I mean . . . just look how tiny we are!

Minuscule oriental rat fleas survive by drinking the blood of other creatures. Usually they feast on rats but sometimes, if they get really hungry, they bite humans instead and pass on the deadly plague-causing bacteria that lives in the rats' blood.

In the fourteenth century they were responsible for the Black Death, a terrible pandemic that began in what is now Kyrgyzstan in central Asia before sweeping down across Europe and North Africa. This plague is estimated to have killed 75 million people and in Europe, nearly half the population died after becoming infected. Because of this, there weren't enough people to farm the land and harvest the crops, which meant many people also died of starvation.

Various plagues struck Europe over the next 300 years. By the seventeenth century, special 'plague doctors' would visit the sick wearing sinister-looking masks with long beaks that were stuffed full of herbs to protect them from infection. These men did their best to treat their patients, but most victims died within a day or two of being bitten. Many of the plague doctors also died. The herbs had a lovely, sweet smell, but they offered no protection at all against the tiny flea.

A Tall Tale

CHINA · 1414

Qilin

I think I am the only giraffe in the whole of China. I've never met another one. I was given to the emperor, Zhu Di, as a gift. He's very kind and introduces me to all the visitors at the palace. Many come just to see me, and many sit and paint pictures of me for hours. I don't think any of them really know what I am . . . they call me 'qilin'. Everyone here makes me feel very special, but I do miss my home. Maybe one day they'll bring another giraffe to the palace for company.

Gifts of rare animals used to be a popular way for kings and queens to impress each other. Rich merchants also sometimes presented exotic beasts to important rulers in order to get permission to trade luxury goods in that country.

The qilin was a gift to Emperor Zhu Di of the Ming dynasty. Qilin was the name of a fabulous mythical beast that the Chinese believed brought good luck to their emperor and to their country. Unlike many earlier Chinese emperors, Zhu Di was interested in building links with other countries and encouraging overseas trade. The giraffe was possibly a gift from one of these merchants, who likely made the long voyage by sea from Africa to Asia before reaching China. Not surprisingly, such a strange-looking beast became a fascinating curiosity for the Chinese, but also a living symbol of international friendship and respect.

During Emperor Zhu Di's reign, he sent more than 300 ships to explore Africa and the Indian Ocean. These are believed to have carried nearly a million tonnes (t) of valuables, such as rare spices, perfumes, gold and gemstones, to trade with countries overseas. One of them may even have brought back a second giraffe for the emperor!

The Dog Who Started a Whole New Church

ENGLAND · 1529

Urian

I am Cardinal Wolsey's most trusted companion and he used to take me on all his travels. Like any good dog, I always do what I can to protect my owner. However, the other day I got in big trouble! The king had sent Wolsey and me to Rome to meet with the pope. But when I came in, my best friend Wolsey was kneeling on the floor and the pope was standing over him. I growled and barked as loudly as I could! Some people say I bit him too . . . but I shouldn't talk about that.

Thomas Wolsey was a butcher's son who became one of the richest and most powerful people in Tudor England. King Henry VIII made him lord chancellor, the country's highest government official, as well as a cardinal – the most important Englishman in the Catholic Church. This was a great honour, until the king and the pope began to argue . . .

Henry wanted to divorce his wife Katherine, but he needed the pope's permission. When the pope refused, the king sent Wolsey to Rome to speak to him, and Wolsey took Urian along for company. When Wolsey knelt to kiss the pope's foot as a sign of respect, Urian panicked, thinking his master was under threat. He growled at the pope, and many say he even bit him. The pope got very angry and Wolsey was sent away without the permission Henry wanted.

The king was furious, and he had Wolsey arrested as a traitor, but the cardinal fell ill and died before he could be locked up in the Tower of London. He was spared the cruel fate of at least 55,000 people who were executed by Henry during his reign, including two of his six wives.

After that, Henry found a different way to get his divorce. He broke away from the Catholic Church and established an entirely new church and appointed himself as its head. Today we call it the Church of England, and – who knows? – without Urian, the story might have been very different.

The President's Royal Gift

UNITED STATES OF AMERICA · 1789

Royal Gift

Today, I had to say farewell to my master, George Washington. When I first arrived from Spain, he had just retired from the army and become a farmer. I always knew that he was someone special because I was given to him by the king of Spain. When people came to visit us on the farm, they treated him with great respect. Some people also called him a hero, which made me proud. I am even prouder today because he has left to become the first president of the United States of America.

American lands had been British colonies for nearly two centuries, until military commander George Washington defeated the British army. As the United States' first president, Washington worked hard to defend the rights of individual citizens and helped make many important laws that are still in force today.

On his farm at Mount Vernon, Washington tested different crops to see which ones were best suited to the USA's soil and climate. He had heard that the best donkeys came from Spain, but no one was allowed to take them out of the country without the king's permission. Both Spain and the USA had been fighting wars against the British, and King Charles III of Spain realised that giving Washington a donkey would be a good way to celebrate the alliance between their two countries.

Washington wanted the donkey so that he could breed it with his horses to produce stronger, healthier animals called mules. These were good for pulling heavy wagons and carrying heavy loads. His plan worked and Royal Gift was sent around the country to encourage other farmers to do the same thing.

Spain's unusual visitor became quite the celebrity. Newspaper advertisements listed the places where Royal Gift would be going, and farmers queued up to borrow him to breed better mules of their own.

But the travelling was exhausting for Royal Gift and from time to time he fell ill. In 1796, the little donkey sickened and died. He is still fondly remembered as the USA's first – and most famous – Spanish donkey.

NEW YORK ILLUSTRATED NEWS

WASHINGTON'S "ROYAL GIFT"

The Pampered Pooch

FRANCE · 1793

Mignon

My name is Thisbe, but the queen always calls me Mignon, which is the French word for 'cute'. I live in a fabulous palace in Paris with Her Majesty and King Louis XVI. We have an even bigger home in the countryside that has over 2,000 rooms and more than 60 staircases to run up and down. There are enormous gardens to enjoy and we are always hosting lavish balls and parties. Well, we were . . . Things have been different recently. I can hear angry voices outside the palace and the queen has started to look a little worried . . .

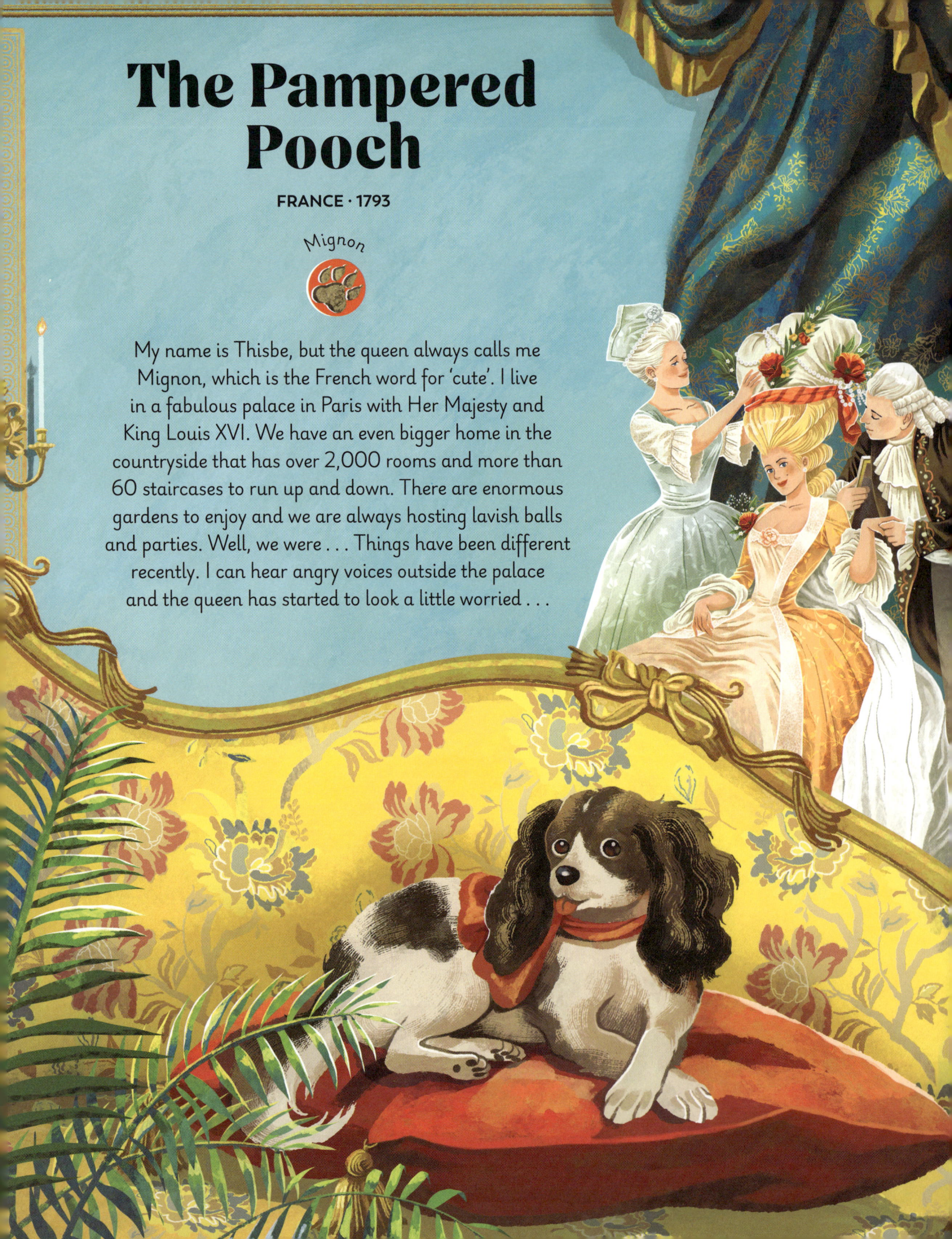

The palace at Versailles was one of the largest and most beautiful buildings in the whole of Europe, but by 1793 the French people were growing tired of King Louis and Marie Antoinette, his extravagant Austrian wife. The pair spent a fortune on silk clothes, fine jewels and beloved pets! They threw grand parties, even though thousands of poor families in Paris were struggling just to buy food.

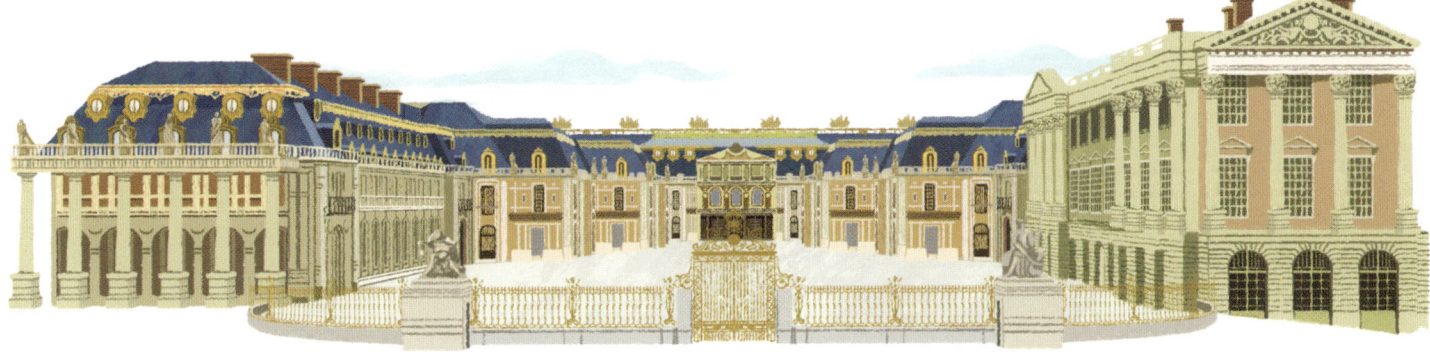

By 1789, the French people began demanding more political power. The king refused and the people's anger soon exploded into violence. This was the beginning of the French Revolution. At first, the revolutionaries called for 'Liberté, Égalité, Fraternité' – meaning freedom, equality and fraternity for everyone – but things rapidly spiralled out of control . . .

During a time the French call 'The Terror', the king was arrested and the monarchy was abolished. Louis was put on trial and executed, using a machine called the guillotine. People were shocked by the brutality of his death but over the next few years, more than a quarter of a million French citizens were arrested for crimes against the revolution. Nearly 17,000 people were beheaded using the same grisly device, often without going to court. Thousands of people were beaten to death on the streets of France.

During the Reign of Terror, Marie Antoinette was locked up in prison. In October 1793, she was finally put on trial and found guilty of treason. Shortly afterwards, Mignon's mistress was beheaded in front of a jeering crowd in Paris. And as for Mignon, he is believed to have been sent to live in Austria with Marie Antoinette's sister.

The Fight for Freedom

UNITED STATES OF AMERICA · 1806

My flock and I have just been bought by a new owner. Farm animals like me are always being traded. But today feels different. My new master bought us, and a young girl named Belle, for a hundred dollars. I'm worried for her. She's young, perhaps eight or nine, and will have to walk a long way back to the farm with us. She looks so tired and scared. I can tell she is dreaming of freedom already.

The early history of the United States is shrouded in slavery. More than 12.5 million Africans were captured and taken by ship across the Atlantic. Nearly 2 million died on the journey, and hundreds of thousands of men and women were forced to work on American farms and plantations.

Their jobs were exhausting and unpaid, and slave owners could be violent and cruel. After she was sold along with a flock of sheep, Belle was treated badly by her new owner. Years later, he sold her to another man who promised to set her free if she worked really hard. But, when he changed his mind, Belle knew she had to escape, even though this meant leaving her son Peter behind. Cruel laws meant Peter belonged not to his mother but to the slave owner.

1828

Belle ran away with her baby daughter Sophia to a town near New York City, but she never forgot Peter. When she heard he had been sold to another farmer, she went to court to try to get him back. The legal arguments were complicated and went on for months, but incredibly, Belle won in the end. It was the first time in American history that a black woman had won a case like this against a white man. Belle changed her name to Sojourner Truth and became an important campaigner for the rights of women and African Americans.

In 1865, slavery was finally abolished in the United States. By then Sojourner was elderly, but she refused to give up fighting for a fairer society. Even in her eighties she was still campaigning for equal rights for women and former enslaved people. When she died in 1883, almost 1,000 people turned up at her funeral to pay their respects.

The Theory of Evolution

GALÁPAGOS ISLANDS (ECUADOR) · 1835

Harriet

A peculiar young man has just arrived on the Galápagos. I wonder where he is from – definitely not these islands. His clothes are too strange, and he looks at us like he's never seen tortoises before. He just sits and watches us, taking notes. I wonder what has brought him here. What is he looking for?

Charles Darwin's visit to the Galápagos changed his life forever. From one small island to the next, Darwin noticed how the plants and animals differed, including the shells of tortoises. Some islands had finches with small beaks, while finches on other islands had long, pointed beaks. Darwin proposed an important new scientific theory that explained how species evolve or change over time.

He called it his 'Theory of Evolution through Natural Selection' and it is still something scientists rely on today. According to Darwin, all living things struggle to survive. Those that are well-suited to their environment have the best chance of surviving. When they have offspring, they pass on their useful characteristics, and this process is repeated through the generations.

Darwin's theory showed how things evolve, but also explained how a species could die out if it is badly suited to the environment. This was controversial in Darwin's day because it went against the Bible story. The Bible says that humans were created by God in his own image, but Darwin showed that they had actually evolved over thousands of years. Darwin became famous but also very unpopular.

When Darwin left the Galápagos, he took thousands of rare plant and animal specimens, including several tortoises. Harriet the tortoise is believed to have been taken to a zoo in Australia. She died in 2006, and was thought to have been 175 years old.

Patriotic Parrot

UNITED KINGDOM · 1851

Coco

My beloved Queen Victoria has many pets . . . but I am her favourite. Especially now that I've learnt how to sing 'God Save the Queen'. I'm part of a big family – Her Majesty already has seven children – and the older ones taught me the words last Christmas. I've been practising ever since and wanted to choose the perfect moment to perform for the queen. Today was the day! She'd just been to the Great Exhibition and was in a fantastic mood. Needless to say, she loved it. She's always found me rather funny.

Queen Victoria and her husband Prince Albert went on to have nine children in all, and Coco the parrot was a noisy and much-loved member of the family.

Prince Albert was industrious and always fascinated by new ideas. He organised a colossal event called the Great Exhibition, an enormous display of objects that celebrated the industry and achievements of people from all around the world.

There were approximately 100,000 exhibits, including many of the most up-to-date inventions as well as amazing natural objects. These included a penknife with 80 blades, a folding piano, a painted fire engine from Canada, tapestries, silks and furniture from France and a lump of gold from Chile that weighed 50 kilograms. The exhibition was held in a magnificent new building nicknamed the 'Crystal Palace' in London's Hyde Park. It was more than a half a kilometre long and so tall that there were gigantic trees growing inside. The building had 293,000 panes of glass, 3,330 iron columns and more than 300 km of metal bars to hold the glass in place.

Tickets cost as little as a shilling (five pence), but when the exhibition closed, it had made so much money that three new museums could be built. Nearly two centuries later, these museums – the Victoria and Albert, Science, and Natural History – are still among London's most popular visitor attractions. They also conduct world-leading research into science, engineering, art and wildlife – including parrots!

The World's Worst Dog Walk
ANTARCTICA · 1911

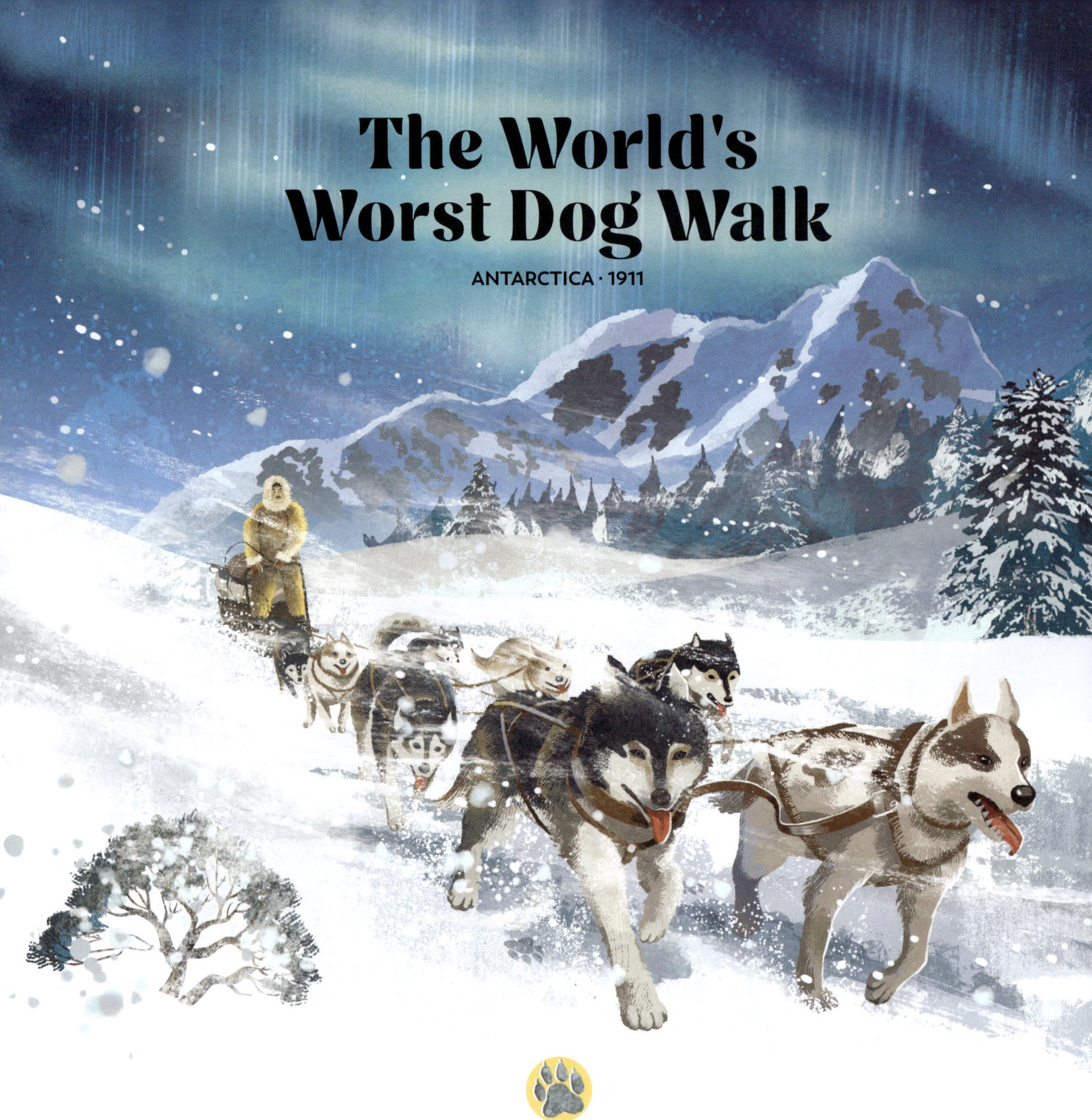

The weather at the South Pole makes it a harsh place even for tough dogs like us. It's cold and windy, and the ice goes on forever. At night, we sleep outside our master's tent. During the day, we pull sledges loaded with supplies across the snow. The guides keep us well fed with fresh seal and penguin. We need it. Our team has a long journey ahead and we need to move quickly. We're determined to be the first team to the South Pole.

The dogs' master was the brilliant Norwegian explorer Roald Amundsen. Today, he is most famous for leading the first team to reach the South Pole – the most desolate, inhospitable spot on the planet.

The adventure began with a sea voyage from Norway. Then when Amundsen set out across the ice, he was accompanied by four other men and dozens of dogs. The dogs included his favourites, Fix and Lassesen, who played a vital role in the expedition's success.

Amundsen's 3,400-km trip across the ice was fraught with danger and took nearly 100 days. Everything he did was planned down to the last detail. He knew, for example, that eating raw meat would stop his men becoming ill with a terrible disease called scurvy. He also chose champion skiers for his expedition team and used knowledge learned from Inuit people, such as wearing fur clothes and how to use the dogs, which he selected and trained. His preparation paid off and Amundsen got his whole team home safely, earning them a place in the history books.

Survivor Pup

ATLANTIC OCEAN · 1912

Sun Yat-sen

My owners and I are looking forward to our trip! We are travelling on a ship called the *Titanic*. It looks enormous, and running around the deck I can see there are plenty of places for me to explore. There are so many people to make a fuss of me – more than 2,400 passengers and nearly 1,000 crew, my mistress says. Lots of them are friendly enough to say hello or pat me on the head and I think a lot of them do it because I'm an unusual type of dog – I'm a Pekingese.

The *Titanic* was a magnificent ocean liner, the largest and most luxurious in the world. It was built using advanced technology, which was supposed to make it fast, and people said it was unsinkable. Its strong hull was made of heavy steel plates and held together by 3 million iron rivets. It was amazingly powerful and an incredible 750 t of coal were needed every day just to fuel the engines driving its three enormous propellers.

But just four days into the *Titanic*'s journey across the Atlantic, a huge iceberg ripped a hole in the great boat's side. Thousands of rivets popped open, thick steel plates were torn apart and hundreds of tonnes of freezing seawater began flooding into the lower decks. It was impossible to repair this sort of damage, so the captain gave the order to abandon ship. In less than three hours, this supposedly unsinkable giant plummeted 3,800 metres (m) down to the sea floor, where it still lies more than a century later.

Sun Yat-sen and his owners Myra and Henry Harper survived the disaster by clambering on to a small wooden lifeboat. Like most other ships at the time, the *Titanic* didn't have enough of these to take everyone on board. Another ship, the *Carpathia*, braved the icebergs and raced to the rescue. Unfortunately, in the several hours it took to reach the *Titanic*, more than 1,500 men, women and children, and many animals, had tragically died in the freezing water.

Deeds Not Words

UNITED KINGDOM · 1913

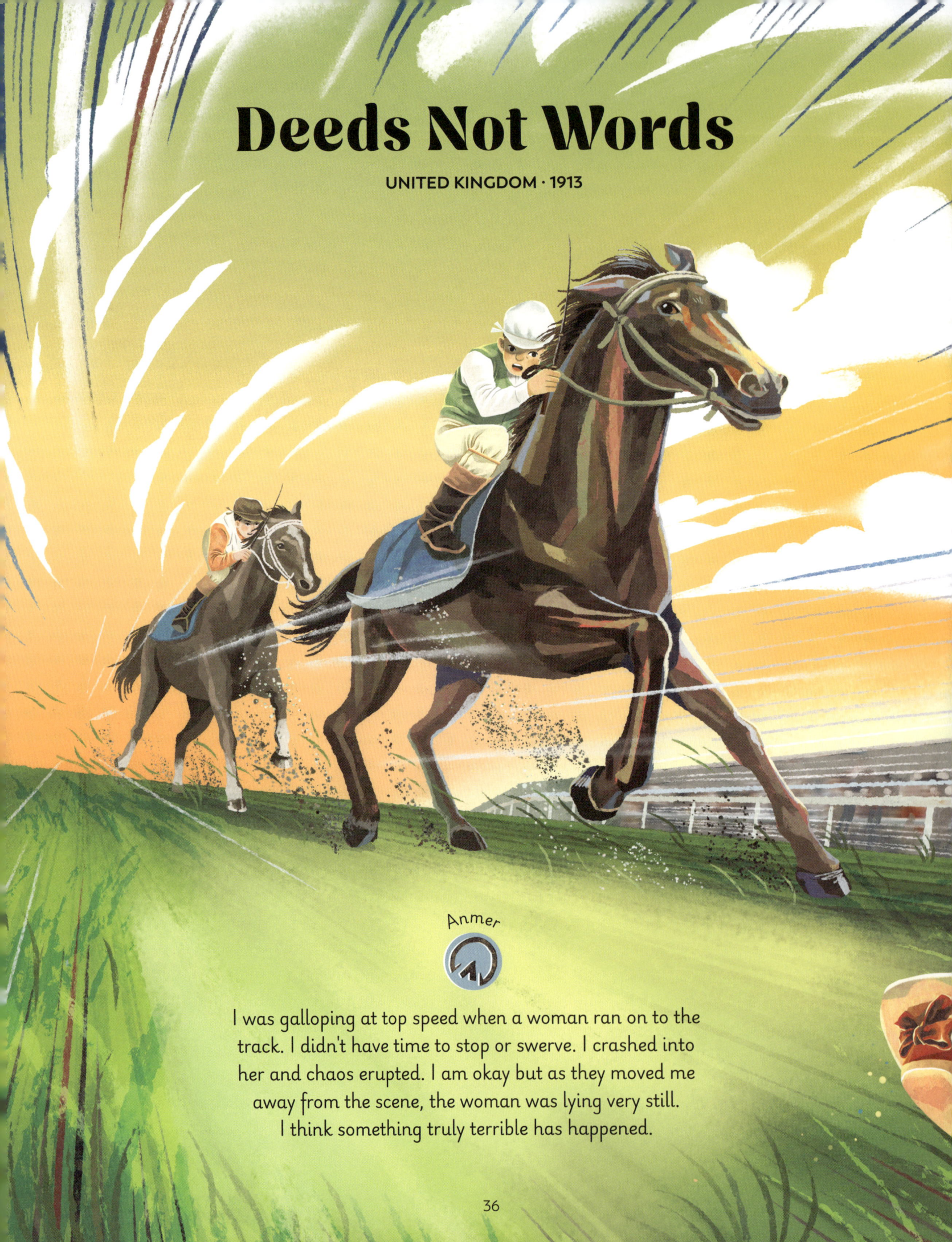

Anmer

I was galloping at top speed when a woman ran on to the track. I didn't have time to stop or swerve. I crashed into her and chaos erupted. I am okay but as they moved me away from the scene, the woman was lying very still. I think something truly terrible has happened.

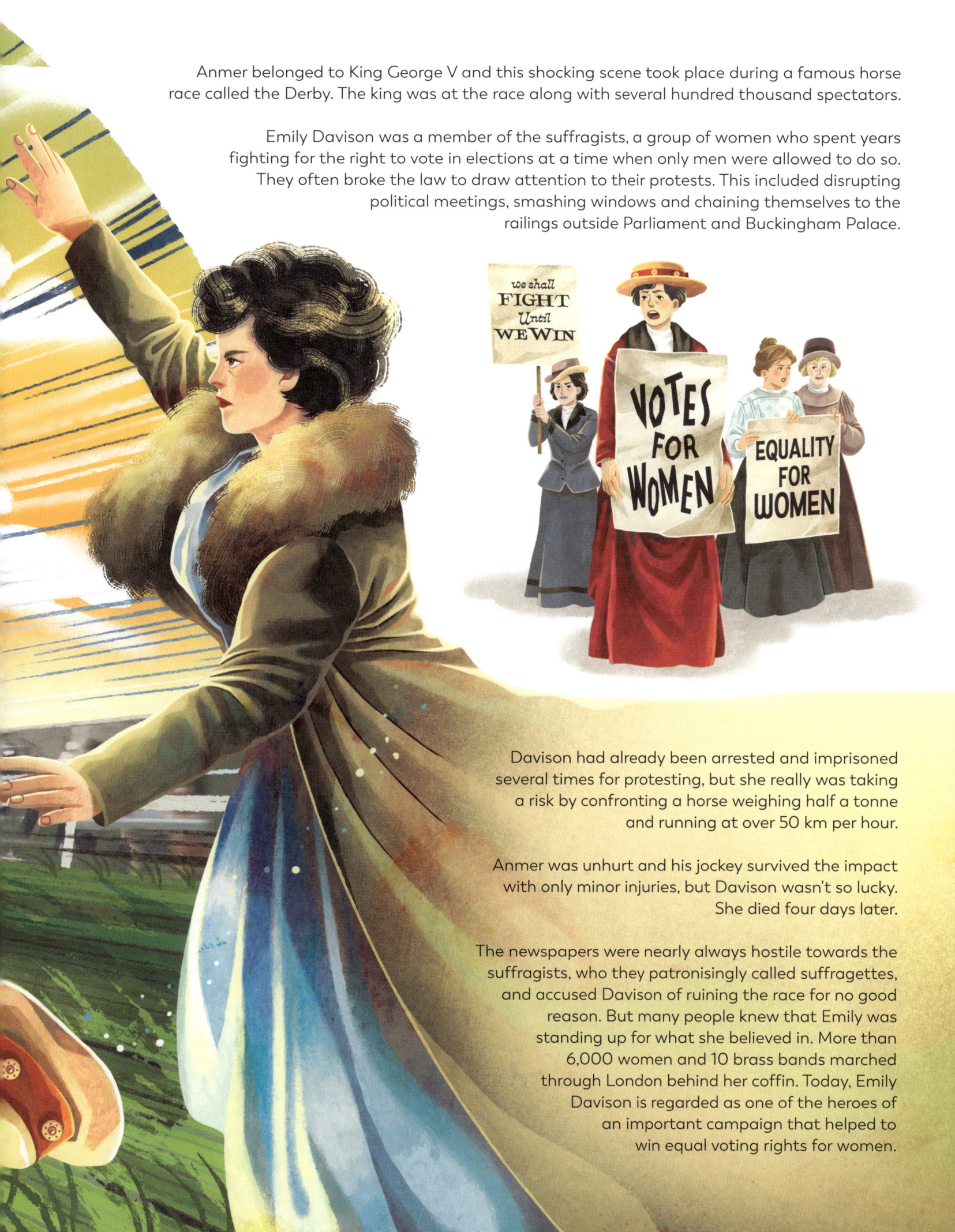

Anmer belonged to King George V and this shocking scene took place during a famous horse race called the Derby. The king was at the race along with several hundred thousand spectators.

Emily Davison was a member of the suffragists, a group of women who spent years fighting for the right to vote in elections at a time when only men were allowed to do so. They often broke the law to draw attention to their protests. This included disrupting political meetings, smashing windows and chaining themselves to the railings outside Parliament and Buckingham Palace.

Davison had already been arrested and imprisoned several times for protesting, but she really was taking a risk by confronting a horse weighing half a tonne and running at over 50 km per hour.

Anmer was unhurt and his jockey survived the impact with only minor injuries, but Davison wasn't so lucky. She died four days later.

The newspapers were nearly always hostile towards the suffragists, who they patronisingly called suffragettes, and accused Davison of ruining the race for no good reason. But many people knew that Emily was standing up for what she believed in. More than 6,000 women and 10 brass bands marched through London behind her coffin. Today, Emily Davison is regarded as one of the heroes of an important campaign that helped to win equal voting rights for women.

Naval May-Ham
THE PACIFIC OCEAN · 1915

Tirpitz

Where are they going? My crew . . . they're sailing away! They will come back and save me, right? Because they're a friendly crew. They always give me big buckets of leftovers to eat. My home, the *Dresden*, has just been attacked by two big British warships and everyone has fled to lifeboats. What's going to happen to me? Oh no – I think a British warship is coming back . . .

Luckily, a British sailor spotted Tirpitz swimming around the wreckage, and she was hauled on to the deck of HMS Glasgow. The pig was given some food and presented with a pretend medal for her bravery.

This happened in 1915, during the First World War. Britain and Germany were enemies, so the British sailors cheekily named their new recruit Tirpitz after one of Germany's senior admirals. Tirpitz became the ship's mascot – she was very lucky, because all the other pigs who came on board were served up as dinner . . .

After a year at sea, Tirpitz was sent to live on a naval base in the south of the United Kingdom. There were plenty of other animals at the base, including chickens, ducks and geese, but the greedy pig was the naughtiest and most annoying animal there. She enjoyed chasing some tame wallabies around their enclosure and frequently broke into the chickens' shed to steal their food. Eventually she was taken away to be sold at a charity auction to raise money for the British Red Cross.

No one knows exactly what happened to Tirpitz, but the war's most famous pig has never been forgotten. After her death, her head was carefully preserved and taken to the Imperial War Museum in London. Visitors may find it curious, even gruesome, but 100 years later it is still on display and very popular.

A Hero's Flight

FRANCE · 1918

Cher Ami

My colleagues need my help. They're trapped behind German lines without any ammunition. But I can save them! You see, pigeons are braver than you think. We fly through smoke and smog, and we keep going even when enemies shower the sky with machine-gun bullets. This mission is dangerous but I know I can do it. I am fast and I can find my way. My talents can save thousands of men, women and children. I'm almost there . . .

Cher Ami was a homing pigeon. These birds have brains smaller than the tip of your finger, but they have a remarkable ability to find their way home. Scientists still haven't completely worked out how they do it, but humans have used pigeons' unique skill to carry urgent updates for centuries.

Good communications are vital in wartime. During the First World War, soldiers, sailors, pilots and even spies began using pigeons to send important messages back to base. The messages were usually written in code and then rolled up and put in tiny metal cylinders that were attached to the birds' legs.

In 1918, when nearly 200 American soldiers became trapped behind German lines without any ammunition, Cher Ami offered their only hope of survival.

The soldiers quickly scribbled an SOS message and put it into Cher Ami's cylinder. The bird flew off at an astonishing 80 km per hour. At once the Germans opened fire. Cher Ami was blinded in one eye, and one bullet badly hurt his right leg. Amazingly, the cylinder containing the message was still attached and, bleeding but determined, Cher Ami kept going.

Twenty-five minutes later, the message was delivered to another platoon more than 65 km away. They quickly organised a rescue mission and the soldiers were saved. Cher Ami also survived his incredible ordeal.

Cher Ami was awarded the Dickin Medal. During the Second World War, several brave animals were awarded medals, and more than half of these were pigeons. It's impossible to say how many lives birds such as Cher Ami saved, but it would be in the thousands.

Feline Friend

NETHERLANDS · 1942

Mouschi

I live in a tiny dark attic with a girl named Anne Frank and her family. There isn't much room at all, and at night-time I snuggle up close to Anne, although we never get much sleep. The noise of bombs exploding outside scares us both, and we often hear men with guns shouting out in the street. Even when it's noisy, Anne's father Otto warns us again and again not to make a sound . . .

When Adolf Hitler and his Nazi Party came to power in Germany in 1933, Jewish people like Anne found themselves in terrible danger. Thousands were imprisoned without trial and others fled their homes before they too were arrested.

Anne's family left home and went to live in Amsterdam in the Netherlands, but after Germany invaded the country in 1940, they were forced into hiding. The Franks squeezed into a tiny secret apartment tucked away behind a warehouse. The family couldn't leave the apartment, even after dark. For nearly two years, they had to keep very quiet to avoid being found. When she was thirteen years old, Anne began keeping a diary. This is how we know so much about her and Mouschi and their hiding place behind the bookshelves.

During Anne's two years in hiding, things got much worse for Jewish people in Europe. The Germans had built thousands of prisons called concentration camps. Whole families were transported to them by train, and many of them were murdered as soon as they arrived.

The Nazis also persecuted Roma people, gay men, disabled people and communists, but by far the largest group in these camps were Jewish men, women and children. Over the course of the Second World War, 6 million Jewish people were murdered.

Tragically, in 1944, someone told the police about the Frank family's hiding place, and they were split up and taken to two of the largest camps, Auschwitz and Bergen-Belsen. When Germany was defeated in 1945, Anne's father Otto was the only member of the family to walk out of the camp alive. Months later, he discovered his daughter's diary had been rescued from the apartment. Anne's story touched the hearts of people all over the world, and her diary has been published in more than 70 languages.

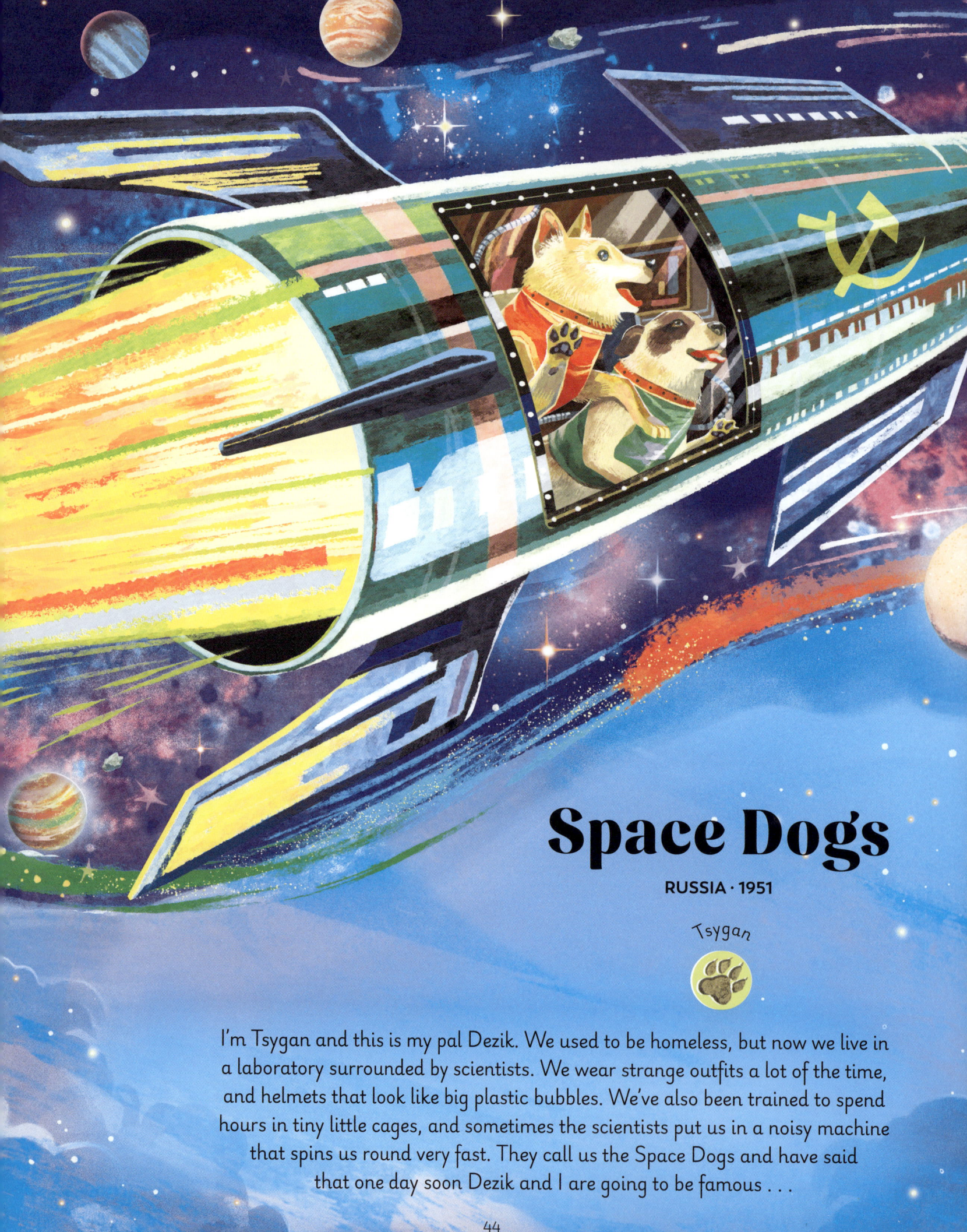

Space Dogs

RUSSIA · 1951

Tsygan

I'm Tsygan and this is my pal Dezik. We used to be homeless, but now we live in a laboratory surrounded by scientists. We wear strange outfits a lot of the time, and helmets that look like big plastic bubbles. We've also been trained to spend hours in tiny little cages, and sometimes the scientists put us in a noisy machine that spins us round very fast. They call us the Space Dogs and have said that one day soon Dezik and I are going to be famous . . .

After the Second World War, the United States and the Soviet Union raced to beat each other into space. Both countries wanted to be the first to walk on the Moon, but before either dared to put humans into rockets, they experimented by blasting animals into space.

The Soviets preferred to send dogs and the first two they sent were named Tsygan and Dezik. The pair were selected because they were strays, and scientists thought they would be tougher and better able to cope.

Tsygan and Dezik went through a period of training, much like human astronauts do now. For much of the time, they were confined to small cages to prepare them for their special dog pods. Being strapped into machines that spun round at high speed was a way to mimic the acceleration of a rocket being launched.

Finally, in 1951, the dogs set foot in a real rocket. These early rockets were unreliable and many had failed to launch properly, but, to everyone's delight, the rocket carrying Tsygan and Dezik successfully reached a height of 110 km before parachuting back to Earth. The dogs were completely unharmed by this extraordinary experience.

A newspaper quickly nicknamed the pair the 'dogmonauts' and both became celebrities around the world, just as the scientists had said they would. Nearly a decade later, another Soviet cosmonaut, Yuri Gagarin, became the first human in space and, eight years after that, the US's Neil Armstrong took the first step on the surface of the Moon.

A True Best Friend

UNITED STATES OF AMERICA · 2001

Roselle

Today began like any other day – my owner Michael and I went to work as usual. Michael is blind and relies on me to guide him to the building where we take the lift up to his office on the 78th floor. I've been sleeping under the desk while he works, but . . . what's that crash? I've just heard an incredibly loud noise from the floor above. The office is filling with smoke and dust. People are telling us to get out . . . I know I have to lead these people to safety.

Michael Hingson worked in the North Tower of New York's World Trade Center, which for a time was the tallest building in the world at 415 m. At 8.45 a.m. a passenger jet crashed into the tower and burst into flames. Shortly afterwards, a second aircraft hit the nearby South Tower. It was a horrific act of terrorism unlike anything that had been seen before.

Inside the buildings, people were desperate to get out, but the lifts in both towers stopped working. Carefully, Roselle the guide dog led Hingson and about 30 of his colleagues towards the stairs.

The stairs were already dangerously overcrowded, and firefighters were rushing up the stairs hoping to stop the fire. Roselle greeted each of them as they passed and managed to remain calm despite the noise and the heat.

It took the group almost an hour to get out of the burning building. When they finally reached the ground, Roselle and Hingson sheltered in a nearby subway station. Moments later, the North Tower collapsed. More than 2,600 people were killed at the World Trade Center that day, including firefighters, police officers and everyone on board the two airliners. But Roselle saved the lives of Hingson and his colleagues.

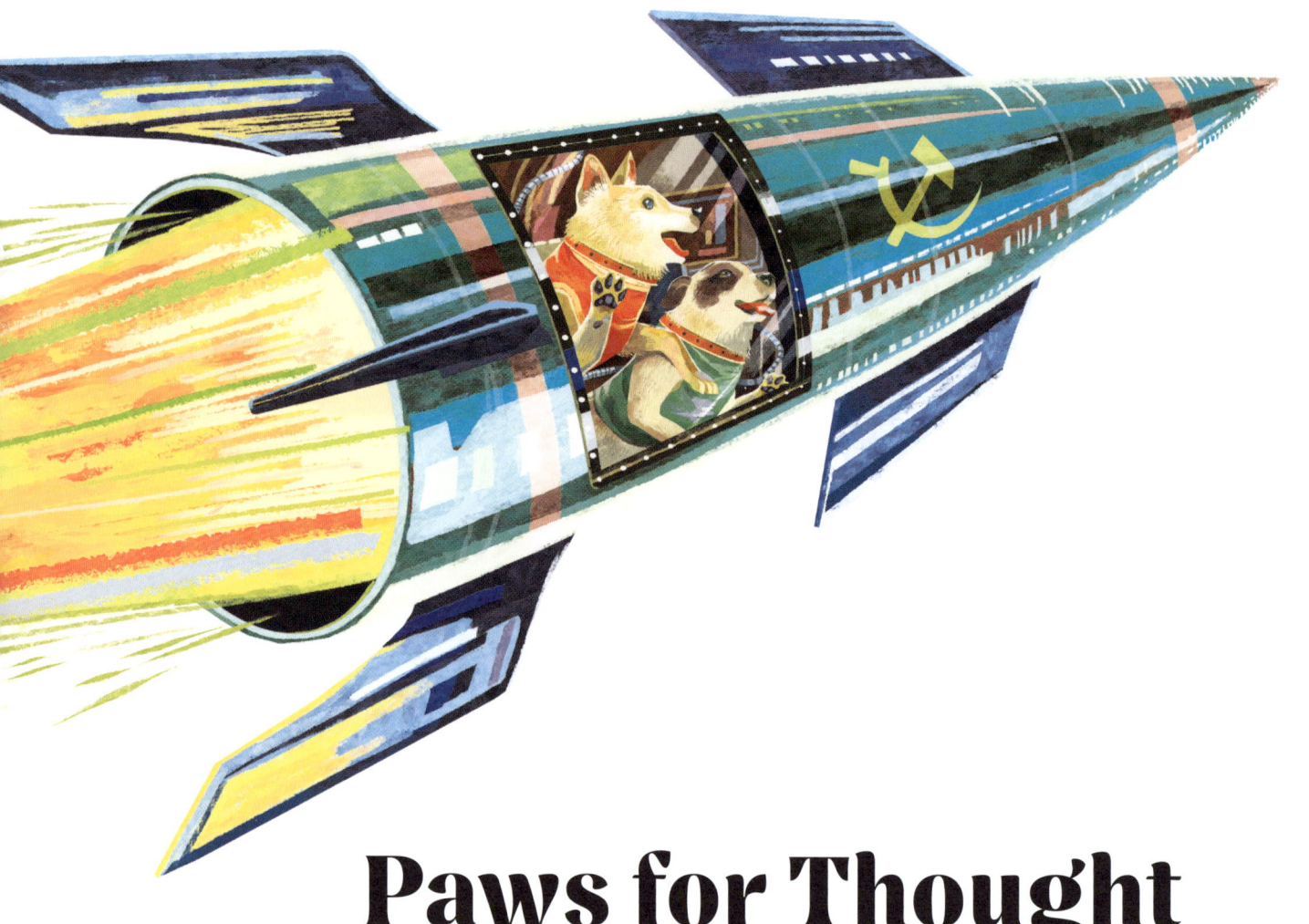

Paws for Thought

It's a mistake to think the past is only about famous people, because they are not the only ones who helped make history. Animals did this too. Tsygan and Dezik rocketed into space years before any humans managed it, and they were followed by numerous cats, ants, flies, frogs and even jellyfish. In the thirteenth century, when the Italian explorer Marco Polo thought he'd found a genuine unicorn, it was really just the first time a European had seen a rhinoceros. And when Mahatma Gandhi led the great struggle to free India from British rule hundreds of years later, he was accompanied everywhere by his goat Nirmala. These days everyone with a pet understands the importance of our relationships with animals, and looking back, we can see this has been true for tens of thousands of years.